· JOHN MALAM ·

Dinosaurs

Atlas in the Round

RUNNING PRESS

PHILADELPHIA · LONDON

Contents

9 8 7 6 5 4 3 2 1
Digit on the right indicates the number of this printing
Library of Congress Cataloging-in-publication number 00 134992
ISBN 0-7624-0965-7

Copyright © 2001 Ivy Press Ltd and
Alastair Campbell
Devised and produced by
Alastair Campbell and The Ivy Press Ltd,
2/3 St Andrews Place, Lewes,
East Sussex BN7 1UP
All rights reserved under the Pan-American
and International Copyright Conventions
Printed in Hong Kong

Art Director: Alastair Campbell
Art Editor: John Carrod
Designer: Rebecca Johns
Managing Editor: Kim Yarwood
Editor: Fid Backhouse
Maps: Nicholas Rowland

This book may be ordered by mail from the publisher. Please include $2.50 for postage and handling. *But try your bookstore first!*

Running Press Book Publishers
125 South Twenty-second Street
Philadelphia, Pennsylvania 19103-4399

Visit us on the web!
www.runningpress.com

Introduction

This book is about a time long ago. It was a time when the world looked different from today, a time when other creatures and plants lived on Earth. Our planet has a long history, and the time described on the following pages is called the Mesozoic era. This means 'middle life'. The Mesozoic was the era before our own time—a time when dinosaurs ruled the Earth.

Blue-green algae

Flat worm

Earth is about 4,600 million years old. For the first 1,000 million years there was no life on the planet. The first life appeared in the sea about 3,500 million years ago. It was blue-green algae that lived in large colonies.

Pterosaur

At first, all life was single-celled (microscopic) and in the sea. There was no life on land. About 600 million years ago the first multi-celled creatures appeared.

By about 550 million years ago more complex creatures had evolved. Some had skeletons and some had shells to support and protect their bodies. Most lived on or near the seabed.

Trilobite

Giant rhinoceros

The first dinosaurs evolved from early reptiles, about 230 million years ago—the Age of Dinosaurs had begun. They lived alongside other creatures, large and small, flyers and swimmers.

An early reptile

When fishes appeared, about 500 million years ago, a major step forward in the evolution of life was made. Fishes were the first vertebrates— creatures with backbones. A backbone strengthens and supports the body.

Armored fish

The Age of Dinosaurs ended about 65 million years ago, and other groups of animals became dominant, such as mammals and birds.

About 290 million years ago, a new group of creatures, called reptiles, evolved from amphibians. They were the first vertebrates to live entirely on the land—there was no need for them to return to the sea.

Woolly mammoth

Millipede

Spiders, millipedes and insects were the first life on land, about 400 million years ago. About 375 million years ago some fishes became amphibians. They led a 'double life', able to live on land and in the sea.

About five million years ago some apes began walking on two feet. From them came the first modern humans, some 200,000 years ago. Animals similar to those we know today lived at this time.

Mesozoic era	PERIOD	MILLIONS OF YEARS AGO	WHAT HAPPENED TO DINOSAURS?
Dinosaurs lived in the Mesozoic era of Earth's history. This era is divided into three smaller parts called periods.	TRIASSIC	250–206 mya	*Time of the first dinosaurs*
	JURASSIC	206–144 mya	*Time of the largest dinosaurs*
	CRETACEOUS	144–65 mya	*Time of the last dinosaurs*

Key to maps
Purple, yellow and red pins show the approximate location of fossil sites, with the fossil's period; blue pins indicate finds for dinosaurs not in this book.

- *Triassic period*
- *Jurassic period*
- *Cretaceous period*
- *Other dinosaur finds, not profiled in book*

Continents on the move

Maps of the world in a modern atlas show us the shapes of the continents and oceans as they appear today. You might think they have always looked like this, and that they have always been in the same positions on the Earth. In fact, the continents have been shaped and moved around over Earth's surface by powerful forces from deep inside the planet.

Many millions of years ago all land on Earth belonged to one huge super-continent. It has been given the name Pangea, meaning 'All Earth'. During the Mesozoic era, Pangea broke up into smaller pieces. They are today's continents. It has taken millions of years for the continents to reach their present-day positions. They are still moving, at an average of about 1½ inches (4 cm) a year.

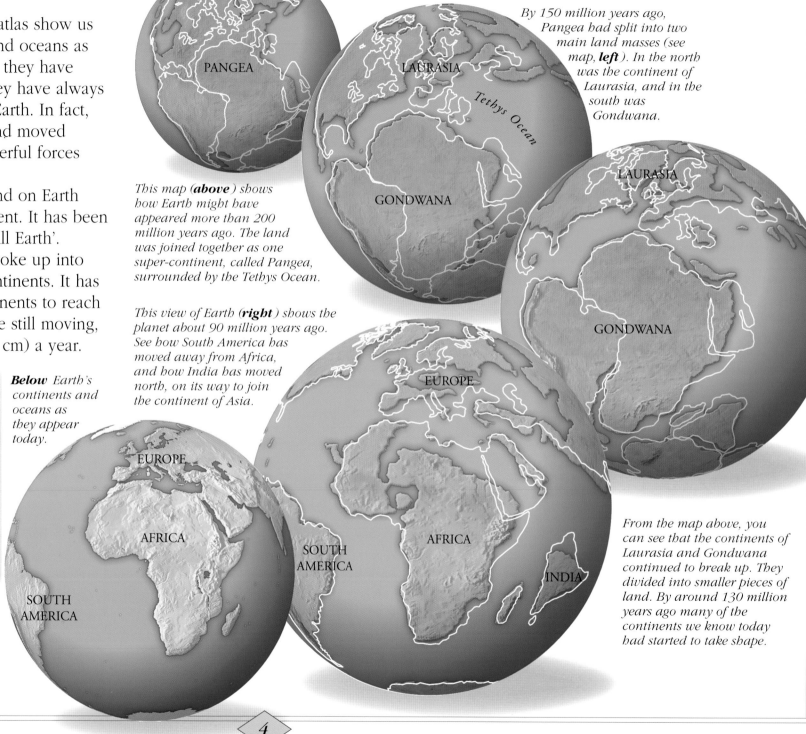

*By 150 million years ago, Pangea had split into two main land masses (see map, **left**). In the north was the continent of Laurasia, and in the south was Gondwana.*

*This map (**above**) shows how Earth might have appeared more than 200 million years ago. The land was joined together as one super-continent, called Pangea, surrounded by the Tethys Ocean.*

*This view of Earth (**right**) shows the planet about 90 million years ago. See how South America has moved away from Africa, and how India has moved north, on its way to join the continent of Asia.*

From the map above, you can see that the continents of Laurasia and Gondwana continued to break up. They divided into smaller pieces of land. By around 130 million years ago many of the continents we know today had started to take shape.

Below *Earth's continents and oceans as they appear today.*

*Continents move because the Earth's top layer, or crust, is divided into pieces called plates. The continents are attached to the plates, and the plates slide on top of Earth's mantle—a layer of molten rock. The places where plates meet can be seen, such as along the San Andreas fault, USA (**above**).*

Triassic period: 250–206 million years ago.

Jurassic period: 206–144 million years ago.

PANGEA

Tethys Ocean

GONDWANA

LAURASIA

Tethys Ocean

GONDWANA

The world the dinosaurs knew

The moving continents are not the only things that made Earth different in the past. The environment was different, too. Each period of the Mesozoic era—the Triassic, Jurassic and Cretaceous— had its own plants and animals. This was the world the dinosaurs knew.

There is another difference between then and now. The first dinosaurs lived when all Earth's land was joined together. They roamed freely across the super-continent. But, as it broke apart, oceans widened to become barriers that dinosaurs could not cross. Dinosaurs became stranded on the continents, and each continent became home to particular types of animal.

EUROPE

Cretaceous period: 144–65 million years ago.

SOUTH AMERICA

Atlantic Ocean

AFRICA

INDIA

Triassic period
The first dinosaurs appeared during the Triassic period. The temperature was warm and dry and conifer and ginkgo trees flourished, as did ferns, horsetails, and cycad plants.

Jurassic period
During the Jurassic period Earth's temperature cooled and rainfall increased. In this moist climate conifer and ginkgo forests spread, and ground-covering plants, such as horsetails and ferns, flourished.

Cretaceous period
Wet and dry seasons developed during the Cretaceous period. The temperature continued to cool and the first flowering plants appeared, as did trees such as oak, maple, and beech.

Dinosaurs at a glance

Dinosaurs were the dominant members of the animal kingdom during the Mesozoic era. However, they were not the only animals that lived on Earth during this long period of the planet's prehistoric past. Dinosaurs shared the world with creatures that flew in the sky and others that swam in the sea. None of these other animals were dinosaurs.

What makes a dinosaur a dinosaur? To be classified as a dinosaur an animal must have lived between 250 million and 65 million years ago, which was the time of the Mesozoic era. It must have lived on land and walked on legs held straight out beneath its body. It must have been a reptile and unable to fly. An animal with all these characteristics was a dinosaur.

Some dinosaurs, such as this Saltasaurus, had long tails

Like other carnivores, Deinonychus probably had good eyesight

A carnivore's tooth

A herbivore's tooth

Dinosaurs may have had distinctive skin colors and patterns

Sight
Carnivores had better sight than herbivores. They needed good sight to see their prey. Some dinosaurs may have been able to see in the dark.

Teeth
Carnivores had curved, blade-like teeth with serrated edges— the ideal meat-cutters. Herbivores had straight peg-like teeth for stripping leaves from branches, and also flatter teeth for chewing and grinding.

Diet
Dinosaurs can be divided into three groups depending on the type of food they ate.

Giganotosaurus

Carnivores were meat-eaters. Predators caught and killed their prey. Scavengers ate meat from animals killed by others.

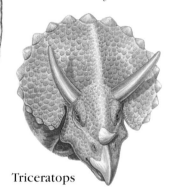

Triceratops

Herbivores were plant-eaters. They ate leaves, stems, fronds, and fruits. Stomach stones helped them digest their food.

Dinosaurs had straight legs beneath their bodies

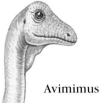

Avimimus

Omnivores had a mixed diet. They ate both meat and plants. They ate fish and eggs, too.

Skin
Dinosaur skin was covered in overlapping scales, like today's reptiles. Some dinosaurs had bony plates, nodules, and spikes embedded in their skin. Others grew feathers over part or all of their bodies.

Feathered dinosaurs
Some dinosaurs may have had feathers, particularly small, agile carnivores such as this Caudipteryx. These so-called 'dinobirds' were unable to fly, but it was from them that modern birds evolved.

Dinosaur families

The animal kingdom is divided into groups, such as reptiles, birds, mammals, and insects. Dinosaurs were reptiles. People who study dinosaurs look for tell-tale features in their fossils. By recognizing the features it is then possible to divide dinosaurs into families. A dinosaur 'family tree' can be made, showing the families and how they are related to each other. The dinosaurs within each family share the same features.

EARLY DINOSAURS

Hip structure

One of the keys to studying dinosaurs lies in the shape of their hip bones. Dinosaurs either had hips with bones shaped like lizards or like birds. Depending on their hip shape, all dinosaurs are divided into either lizard-hipped (saurischian) or bird-hipped (ornithischian) dinosaurs.

Right: *A simplified 'family tree'. Dinosaurs trace their origins back to a common ancestor. As they evolved, they branched out. One branch, birds, continues to the present day.*

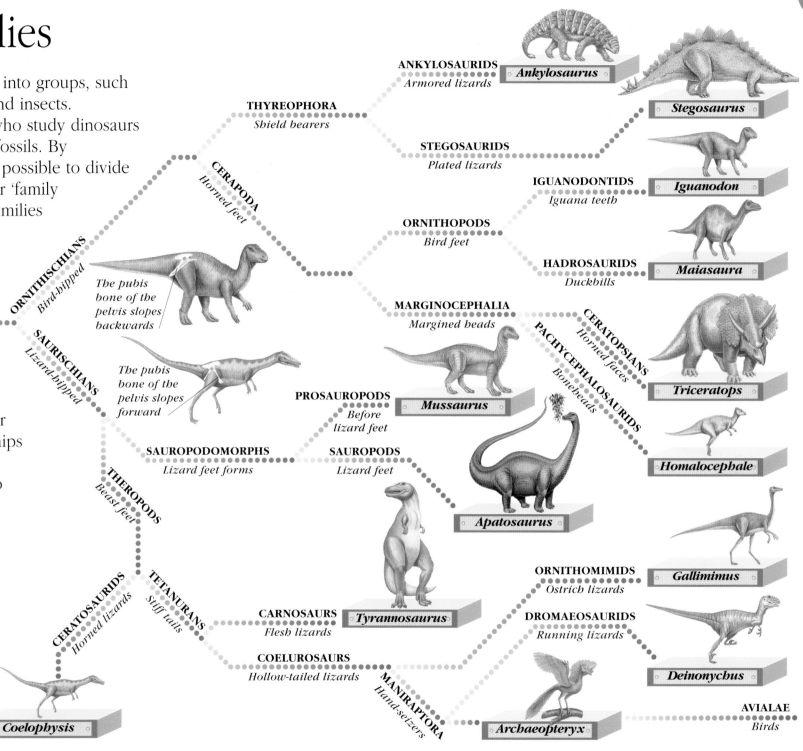

ORNITHISCHIANS
Bird-hipped

The pubis bone of the pelvis slopes backwards

The pubis bone of the pelvis slopes forward

SAURISCHIANS
Lizard-hipped

CERAPODA
Horned feet

THYREOPHORA
Shield bearers

ANKYLOSAURIDS
Armored lizards

Ankylosaurus

STEGOSAURIDS
Plated lizards

Stegosaurus

ORNITHOPODS
Bird feet

IGUANODONTIDS
Iguana teeth

Iguanodon

HADROSAURIDS
Duckbills

Maiasaura

MARGINOCEPHALIA
Margined heads

CERATOPSIANS
Horned faces

PACHYCEPHALOSAURIDS
Boneheads

Triceratops

Homalocephale

PROSAUROPODS
Before lizard feet

Mussaurus

SAUROPODOMORPHS
Lizard feet forms

SAUROPODS
Lizard feet

Apatosaurus

THEROPODS
Beast feet

CERATOSAURIDS
Horned lizards

TETANURANS
Stiff tails

CARNOSAURS
Flesh lizards

Tyrannosaurus

COELUROSAURS
Hollow-tailed lizards

MANIRAPTORA
Hand-seizers

ORNITHOMIMIDS
Ostrich lizards

Gallimimus

DROMAEOSAURIDS
Running lizards

Deinonychus

AVIALAE
Birds

Archaeopteryx

Coelophysis

Dinosaurs in North America

The dinosaurs found in North America, particularly in the United States, are among the best known in the world. There are two main reasons for this.

First, in some areas, such as the western region of the USA, the climate is dry, there is little vegetation covering the bedrock and there are large expanses of rock outcrops. As natural erosion wears the rock away, fossils are gradually exposed.

The second reason is that dinosaur fossils have been collected and studied here since the 1850s. Now, the continent is home to some of the world's leading dinosaur experts and museums.

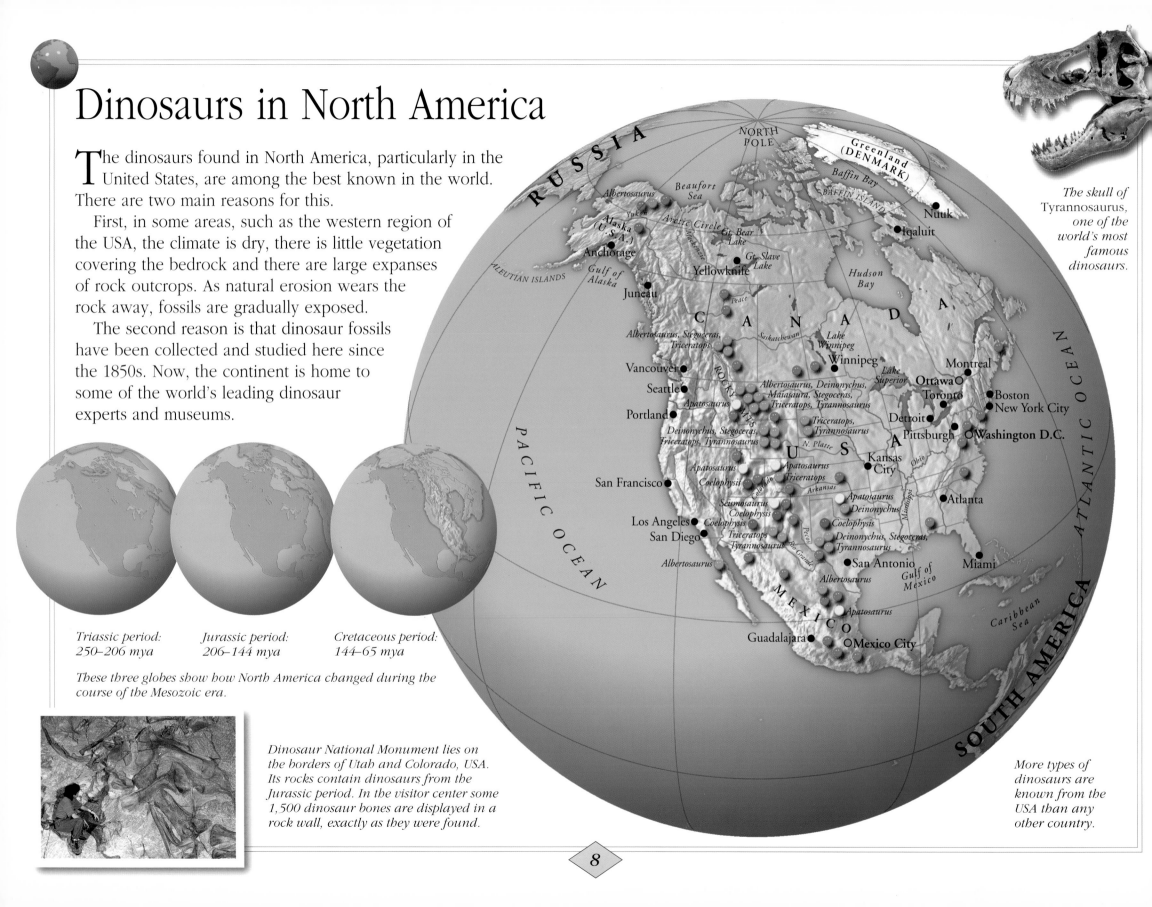

The skull of Tyrannosaurus, one of the world's most famous dinosaurs.

Triassic period: 250–206 mya

Jurassic period: 206–144 mya

Cretaceous period: 144–65 mya

These three globes show how North America changed during the course of the Mesozoic era.

Dinosaur National Monument lies on the borders of Utah and Colorado, USA. Its rocks contain dinosaurs from the Jurassic period. In the visitor center some 1,500 dinosaur bones are displayed in a rock wall, exactly as they were found.

More types of dinosaurs are known from the USA than any other country.

● ALBERTOSAURUS *al-bur-toh-sore-us*

Length: *30 ft (9 m)*   **Weight:** *2 tons*

Lived: *70 million years ago (Late Cretaceous)*

Albertosaurus ('Alberta Lizard') was a strongly built meat-eater, and was a relative of *Tyrannosaurus*. It had many of the features common to other tyrannosaurids ('tyrant lizards'). It had a massive head, its jaws were packed with long, sharp teeth, its body was compact and its hind legs contained strong muscles which gave it the power to run fast. Like other members of its family, its arms were small and each hand had two fingers. Perhaps it used these tiny limbs to grip prey while it bit and kicked its victim.

● *It preyed on slow-moving, small animals which it chased at up to 19 mph (30 km/h).*

● *As its eyes were on the sides of its head it might have had difficulty seeing anything straight in front of it.*

● *To make up for poor eyesight, it may have had a very good sense of smell.*

Teeth had serrated edges to cut through meat

Short, compact body

The flexible tail helped to balance its heavy body

Short arms, each with two fingers on the hand

Three big clawed toes on each foot

Albertosaurus *from:* Canada, Mexico, USA (*Alaska, Montana*).

The long, whip-like tail could be flicked at an attacker

A small head on a long, flexible neck

Massive, pillar-like legs, with hind legs longer than front legs

Apatosaurus *from:* Mexico, USA (*Colorado, Montana, Oklahoma, Utah*).

● APATOSAURUS *ah-pat-oh-sore-us*

Length: *69 ft (21 m)*   **Weight:** *30 tons*

Lived: *150 million years ago (Late Jurassic)*

A giant plant-eating dinosaur, *Apatosaurus* ('Deceptive Lizard') was a slow-moving animal. It may have spent much of the time eating in order to keep its huge body alive. Leaves, which it could take from the tops of trees, and horsetails and ferns on the ground were probably its main sources of food. In the front of its mouth were teeth shaped like pegs. There were no teeth at the back of its mouth. By combing its teeth through vegetation it could strip away the soft parts it wanted to eat, leaving tougher parts behind. The tongue pushed food to the back of its mouth, ready to swallow whole.

● *It swallowed stones, called gastroliths, which crushed plant material inside its stomach into a digestible pulp.*

● *It used to be called Brontosaurus ('Thunder Lizard').*

● COELOPHYSIS *see-loh-fie-sis*

Length: *10 ft (3 m)*   **Weight:** *88 lb (40 kg)*

Lived: *220 million years ago (Late Triassic)*

A small, agile creature, *Coelophysis* ('Hollow Form') was a meat-eater that might have lived and hunted in packs. Its leg bones were almost hollow—hence its name—which would have reduced its weight. With a lightweight body, *Coelophysis* could have run faster and further than its rivals. It probably ate small vertebrates, fish, and insects.

● *Hundreds of Coelophysis skeletons have been found in one place in New Mexico, USA. They may have been a herd that drowned when a river flooded and trapped them.*

● *A Coelophysis skeleton with the bones of a baby Coelophysis inside it suggests this dinosaur might have been a cannibal.*

A long, slim head, large eyes and many small, sharp teeth

Coelophysis *from:* USA (*Arizona, New Mexico, Texas, Utah*).

DEINONYCHUS *die-non-ick-us*

Length: *10 ft (3 m)*   **Weight:** *176 lb (80 kg)*

Lived: *110 million years ago (Early Cretaceous)*

Deinonychus ('Terrible Claw') earned its name from the large, sickle-shaped claw on the second toe of each foot. In an adult these claws were 5 in (13 cm) long. When it walked or ran, it held the claws upright, to prevent them rubbing on the ground and wearing down. It was when the meat-eating *Deinonychus* went in search of prey that it put its deadly claws to use. With their sharp points and edges, these blade-like claws would have sliced deep into a victim's body. *Deinonychus* might have hunted in packs, stalking a creature much larger than itself until rushing in for the kill. It may have held onto its prey to weaken it.

● *Its jaws were packed with sharp teeth. Since they pointed backwards this would have made it difficult for a victim to pull free of them without causing itself greater injury.*

Deinonychus *from:* USA *(Montana, Oklahoma, Texas, Wyoming)*.

Large eyes for good vision

Short arms

Perhaps its skin was patterned to camouflage it

'Terrible claw'

SEISMOSAURUS *size-moh-sore-us*

Length: *131 ft (40 m)*   **Weight:** *30 tons*

Lived: *150 million years ago (Late Jurassic)*

Seismosaurus ('Earth-Shaking Lizard') was one of the largest dinosaurs. A giant plant-eater, it was a member of the diplodocid ('double-beam') family. This means that some of its tail bones had pairs of bony projections ('beams') on either side of them. Perhaps these bones gave added support to the animal's long, flexible tail. Like other sauropods (long-necked, long-tailed plant-eaters) *Seismosaurus* had stomach stones (gastroliths) in its belly. Without chewing teeth, these stones crushed its food to a pulp, making it easier to digest.

● *Only one* Seismosaurus *has been found. In its stomach was a pile of nearly 250 gastroliths, each about 2 in (5 cm) in size.*

● *A fully grown, healthy* Seismosaurus *probably had few enemies—a creature so big would have been difficult to attack.*

Maiasaura *from:* USA *(Montana)*.

Long head

The young may have recognized a parent by distinctive body markings and by calls

Strong fingers were used to hollow out a nest in the soil

MAIASAURA *may-ah-sore-ah*

Length: *30 ft (9 m)*   **Weight:** *3 tons*

Lived: *80 million years ago (Late Cretaceous)*

More is known about *Maiasaura* ('Good Mother Lizard') than many dinosaurs. This is because hundreds of well-preserved specimens have been found at a nest site, from eggs and babies to juveniles and adults. With so much material to study, it has been possible to work out the life-cycle of *Maiasaura* from birth to death. Its lifestyle has been investigated, too. It was a hadrosaurid ('duck-billed') dinosaur. Members of this family had wide, flat beaks. There were no teeth at the front of the mouth, but there were many small cheek teeth. It was a plant-eater that lived in very large herds.

● *It was named 'Good Mother' because it cared for its young. Babies were born in well-made nests and parents brought food to them.*

● *A fully grown adult* Maiasaura *ate about 200 lb (90 kg) of vegetation every day.*

'Double-beam' bones in this part of its tail

Front legs shorter than back legs

A long, flexible neck, able to reach to the tops of tall conifer and ginkgo trees

Pillar-like legs

Seismosaurus *from:* USA *(New Mexico)*.

Stegoceras *from:*
Canada, USA
(*Montana, Texas,
Wyoming*).

*The bone of its skull
was almost 2½ in
(6 cm) thick*

*Long,
stiff tail*

Short arms

● STEGOCERAS *steg-oh-ser-as*

Length: *6 ft (2 m)* **Weight:** *121 lb (55 kg)*

Lived: *70 million years ago (Late Cretaceous)*

A pachycephalosaurid ('bone-headed') dinosaur, *Stegoceras* ('Horny Roof') had many things in common with other members of its family. It was a plant-eater, whose large, thick-boned skull was its most distinctive feature. It was once thought it used its skull to head-butt

other animals—but this might have done it more harm than good. Perhaps it used its head to push and shove an opponent, to decide who was the stronger of the two. Animals often use displays of strength to determine who should be the leader of a group.

● *Its small size and long hind legs suggest that* Stegoceras *was a fast mover, able to sprint away from danger.*

● *The back of its skull was covered with bony knobs and bumps. This feature is called a skull shelf.*

*Long hind
legs, each
with four
toes*

Triceratops *from:*
Canada, USA
(*Colorado,
Montana, New
Mexico, South
Dakota, Wyoming*).

*Bone neck frill
edged with
bony nodules*

*In short bursts
of speed it may
have reached
30 mph
(48 km/h)*

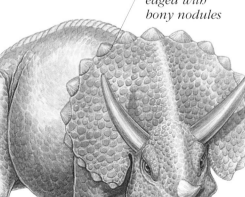

● TRICERATOPS *try-ser-a-tops*

Length: *30 ft (9 m)* **Weight:** *5 tons*

Lived: *70 million years ago (Late Cretaceous)*

The plant-eating *Triceratops* ('Three-horned Face') belonged to the ceratopsid ('horn-faced') group of dinosaurs. These were some of the last dinosaurs to live on Earth, and *Triceratops* was one of the most striking of them. Its bulky body was carried near to the ground on four short legs. From the back of its skull grew a wide frill of solid bone—a shield that protected its unarmored body. On the front of its skull were three long horns, each of which could pierce the skin of a meat-eating predator. If it was threatened, it might have used its neck frill and horns in a show of aggression to scare its attacker away.

● *On a fully grown adult* Triceratops, *the horns that grew on its brow were up to 3 ft (1 m) long.*

● *Its jaws ended in a large bony beak that would have been used to nip and tug at vegetation, such as the tough fronds of cycads and palm trees.*

● TYRANNOSAURUS *tie-ran-oh-sore-us*

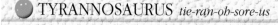

Length: *40 ft (12 m)* **Weight:** *8 tons*

Lived: *70 million years ago (Late Cretaceous)*

Tyrannosaurus ('Tyrant Lizard') was one of the largest of all meat-eating predatory dinosaurs. It had a range of features which gave it many advantages over creatures less fortunate than itself. It had the power of speed, able to stride after its prey at up to 23 mph (36 km/h). It probably had a keen sense of smell, and good eyesight. But its jaws were its most dangerous assets. They were controlled by strong muscles that gave *Tyrannosaurus* a powerful bite. And when it bit into its prey, its long knife-like teeth—each up to 7 in (18 cm) long—sliced deep into the victim's flesh. It then shook its head from side to side, tearing off a chunk of meat.

● *When it walked or ran, it held its body level with the ground and its tail straight out behind it for balance.*

● *Like modern meat-eating animals,* Tyrannosaurus *probably gorged itself on its prey, then went for several days before needing to eat again.*

*New teeth
formed as
worn ones fell
out through
old age, or
were broken*

*Like other tyrannosaurids
it had short arms and two
fingers on each hand*

Tyrannosaurus *from:*
USA (*Montana, New
Mexico, South
Dakota, Texas,
Wyoming*).

*Heavily built hind legs
and three-toed feet*

Dinosaurs in South America

Until the 1950s little had been done to discover which dinosaurs had lived on the continent of South America. Since then, many important discoveries have been made. Scientists now know that dinosaurs lived in South America for about 165 million years—almost the whole of the Mesozoic era.

Some 50 species of dinosaur are now known from the continent, including one of the world's oldest-known dinosaurs, *Eoraptor*, and one of the world's largest meat-eater, *Giganotosaurus*.

More species of dinosaur have been found in Argentina than in any other part of South America. This is because most work has been done here. However, dinosaurs lived across the continent and as more work is done they will be found in other countries.

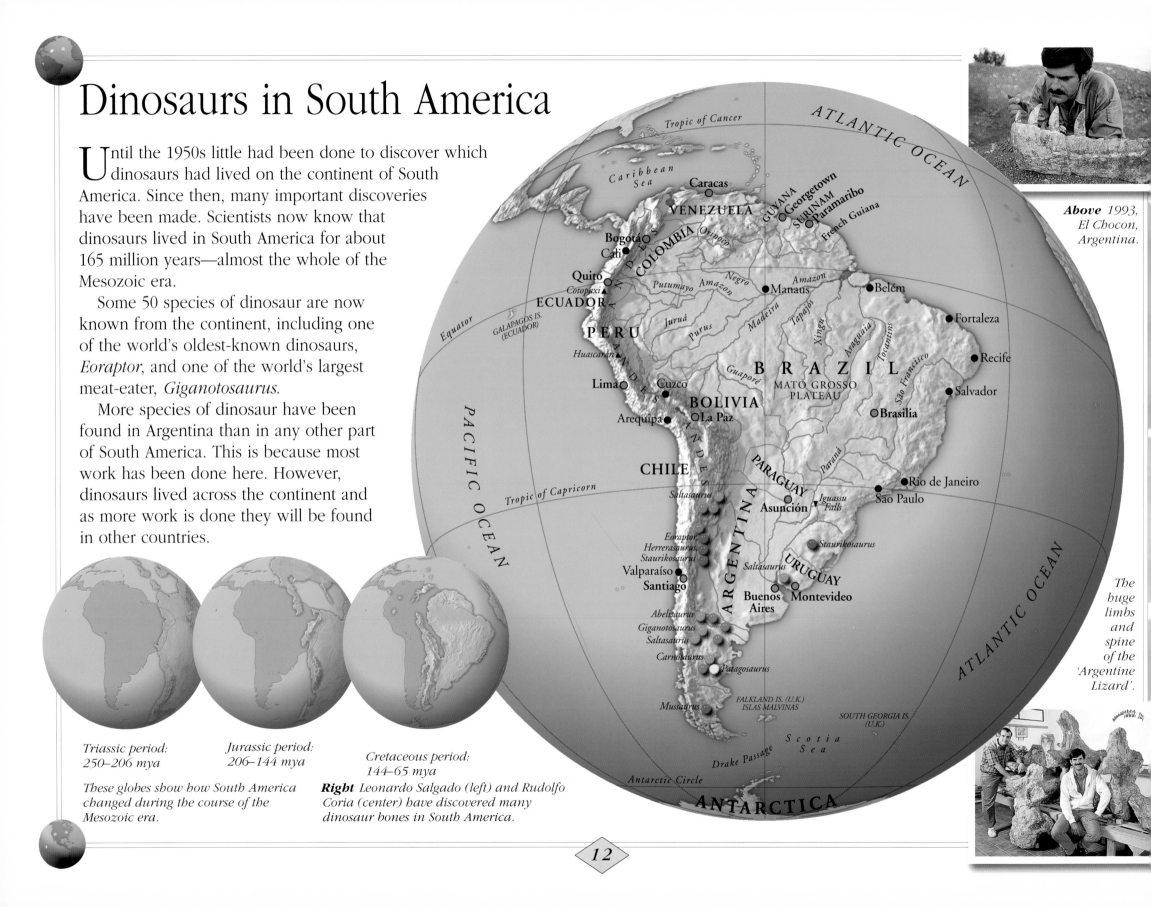

Above 1993, El Chocon, Argentina.

The huge limbs and spine of the 'Argentine Lizard'.

Triassic period: 250–206 mya

Jurassic period: 206–144 mya

Cretaceous period: 144–65 mya

These globes show how South America changed during the course of the Mesozoic era.

Right Leonardo Salgado (left) and Rudolfo Coria (center) have discovered many dinosaur bones in South America.

Abelisaurus *from:*
Argentina.

*Only the 35 inch-
long (90 cm) skull
of Abelisaurus has
so far been found.*

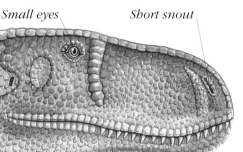

Small eyes

Short snout

Long, slender teeth

 CARNOTAURUS *car-no-tor-us*

Length: *21 ft (6.5 m)*	Weight: *1 ton*

Lived: *95 million years ago (Early Cretaceous)*

Like other dinosaurs from South America, *Carnotaurus* ('Meat Bull') was unlike those from elsewhere in the world. It, too, had followed its own course of evolution, developing unique characteristics not shared by other dinosaurs. Without a doubt, its most distinctive feature was a pair of bony horns that grew from its skull, just above its small eyes. Perhaps they were used in head-butting contests against other members of its species. A meat-eater that walked on two legs, *Carnotaurus* may not have been as fearsome as its name suggests. Even though its large head looks formidable, its jaws and teeth were rather weak.

 The single specimen found so far is remarkable because an impression of the creature's skin has been well preserved. It shows that its body was covered with disc-shaped scales.

 Like other meat-eaters its arms were short— but those of Carnotaurus were shorter than those of most others.

 ABELISAURUS *ah-bell-i-sore-us*

Length: *23 ft (7 m)*	Weight: *1.5 tons*

Lived: *70 million years ago (Late Cretaceous)*

Some dinosaurs are found only in South America and nowhere else on Earth. This is particularly true of the dinosaurs that lived there during the Cretaceous period. By this time South America had moved far enough away from other land to become a continent in its own right. Dinosaurs that lived there evolved as distinct species, related to dinosaurs elsewhere in the world but no longer identical to them. One of these was *Abelisaurus* ('Abel's Lizard'), whose 'distant cousin' was the two-legged meat-eater *Albertosaurus*, from North America.

 A feature that identifies Abelisaurus as a distinct species, different from other large meat-eaters, is a partially closed-off eye socket (the hole in the skull where the eyes sits is partly filled with bone).

 Abelisaurus has been called 'old-fashioned'. This is because some of its features, such as its eye socket, are quite primitive. They are found in dinosaurs that died out before Abelisaurus lived.

Horns above
eyes

Thin
teeth

Slender
lower jaw

 EORAPTOR *ee-oh-rap-tor*

Length: *3 ft (1 m)*	Weight: *6½ lb (3 kg)*

Lived: *228 million years ago (Late Triassic)*

Discovered in 1991, in northwest Argentina, *Eoraptor* ('Dawn Thief') was then the world's oldest-known dinosaur. It lived right at the beginning of the Age of Dinosaurs. It was a small dinosaur that moved swiftly around on two long, slender hind legs. A meat-eater that may have been both a hunter and a scavenger, its long jaws were packed with many small, serrated teeth. The area where its fossils have been found was a river valley during the Triassic period. Perhaps it hunted the area's fish and insects.

 Because some of its bones were hollow, Eoraptor had a very lightweight body.

 It had about 70 bones in its backbone and the legs were twice as long as the arms.

Eoraptor *from:*
Argentina.

Lightly built body

Long
snout

Short arms with
five fingers

Long, thin legs with three-toed feet

Distinctive skin
composed of non-
overlapping scales

Carnotaurus
from:
Argentina.

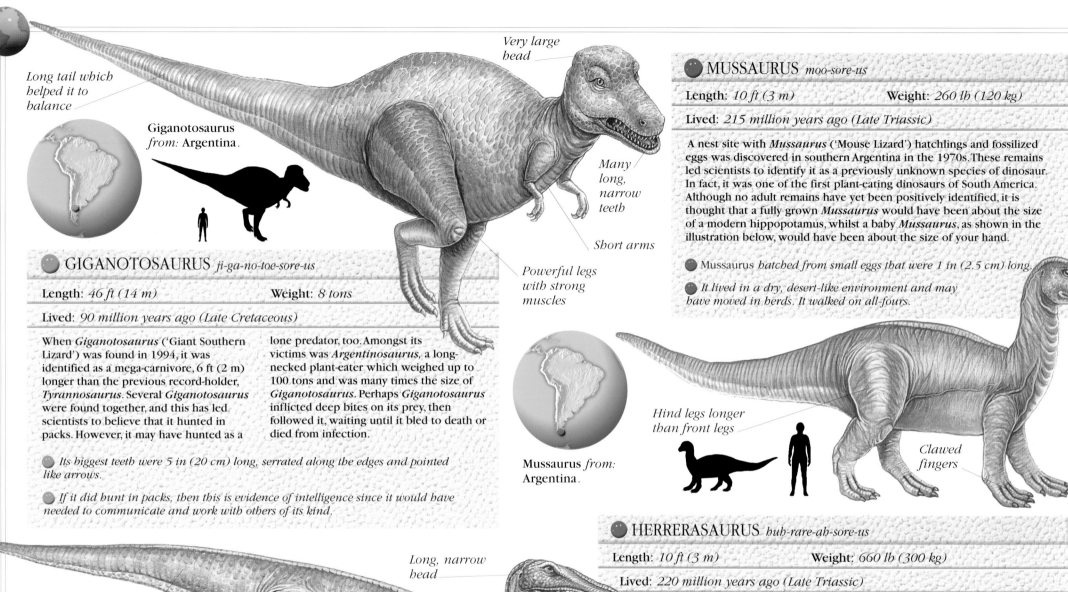

Long tail which helped it to balance

Very large head

Giganotosaurus from: Argentina.

Many long, narrow teeth

Short arms

Powerful legs with strong muscles

● MUSSAURUS *moo-sore-us*

Length: *10 ft (3 m)* **Weight:** *260 lb (120 kg)*

Lived: *215 million years ago (Late Triassic)*

A nest site with *Mussaurus* ('Mouse Lizard') hatchlings and fossilized eggs was discovered in southern Argentina in the 1970s. These remains led scientists to identify it as a previously unknown species of dinosaur. In fact, it was one of the first plant-eating dinosaurs of South America. Although no adult remains have yet been positively identified, it is thought that a fully grown *Mussaurus* would have been about the size of a modern hippopotamus, whilst a baby *Mussaurus*, as shown in the illustration below, would have been about the size of your hand.

● *Mussaurus batched from small eggs that were 1 in (2.5 cm) long.*

● *It lived in a dry, desert-like environment and may have moved in herds. It walked on all-fours.*

● GIGANOTOSAURUS *ji-ga-no-toe-sore-us*

Length: *46 ft (14 m)* **Weight:** *8 tons*

Lived: *90 million years ago (Late Cretaceous)*

When *Giganotosaurus* ('Giant Southern Lizard') was found in 1994, it was identified as a mega-carnivore, 6 ft (2 m) longer than the previous record-holder, *Tyrannosaurus*. Several *Giganotosaurus* were found together, and this has led scientists to believe that it hunted in packs. However, it may have hunted as a lone predator, too. Amongst its victims was *Argentinosaurus*, a long-necked plant-eater which weighed up to 100 tons and was many times the size of *Giganotosaurus*. Perhaps *Giganotosaurus* inflicted deep bites on its prey, then followed it, waiting until it bled to death or died from infection.

● *Its biggest teeth were 5 in (20 cm) long, serrated along the edges and pointed like arrows.*

● *If it did hunt in packs, then this is evidence of intelligence since it would have needed to communicate and work with others of its kind.*

Hind legs longer than front legs

Clawed fingers

Mussaurus from: Argentina.

● HERRERASAURUS *huh-rare-ah-sore-us*

Length: *10 ft (3 m)* **Weight:** *660 lb (300 kg)*

Lived: *220 million years ago (Late Triassic)*

Herrerasaurus ('Herrera's Lizard') was one of the first dinosaurs. It lived during the earliest period of the Mesozoic Era, and was at home among ferns and conifer trees. A meat-eater, *Herrerasaurus* was a fast-moving predator. Its long legs gave it the ability to chase prey, such as rhynchosaurs (plant-eating reptiles) that were the predominant animals on land. Though small, *Herrerasaurus* had similar features to the larger carnivores that lived after it. Like them, it had strong jaws packed with backward-pointing sharp teeth, small arms and a long tail. These features helped to make it one of the most successful dinosaurs of its time.

● *The first* Herrerasaurus *specimen was discovered in 1958 by a farmer called Victorino Herrera, after whom it was named. Others have been found since.*

● *Because* Herrerasaurus *was an early dinosaur, some of its features, such as its leg and feet bones, were primitive compared with those of later dinosaurs.*

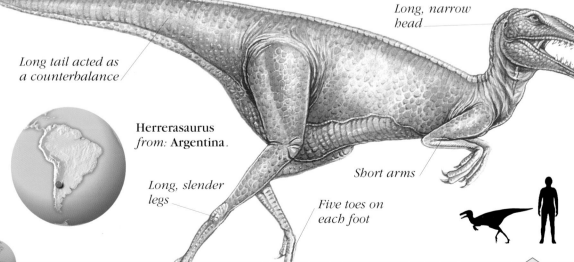

Long tail acted as a counterbalance

Long, narrow head

Herrerasaurus from: Argentina.

Long, slender legs

Short arms

Five toes on each foot

PATAGOSAURUS *pa-ta-go-sore-us*

Length: *65 ft (20 m)* **Weight:** *15 tons*

Lived: *165 million years ago (Middle Jurassic)*

From Patagonia—the southern tip of Argentina—comes *Patagosaurus* ('Patagonian Lizard'). Very few large plant-eating dinosaurs have been found in South America, which makes *Patagosaurus* something of a rarity. It lived at a time when South America was still connected in part to western Europe and Africa. Dinosaurs could travel between these regions, but as the continents drifted apart the land bridge disappeared beneath the ocean. *Patagosaurus* is similar to a dinosaur from Europe, *Cetiosaurus*. They may have had the same ancestor, which is evidence that the land was once joined.

● *The very large and slow-moving* Patagosaurus *would have made an easy target for predators. It may have used its long tail to lash out at them.*

● *Like other giant plant-eaters,* Patagosaurus *walked on all fours. It had a long neck and, for reasons of safety, may have lived in herds.*

Small skull

Shoulder joint

Elbow joint

Wrist joint

Backbone

Ribs

Hip

Knee joint

Ankle joint

Patagosaurus *from:* Argentina.

SALTASAURUS *sal-ta-sore-us*

Length: *40 ft (12 m)* **Weight:** *20 tons*

Lived: *80 million years ago (Late Cretaceous)*

This dinosaur is notable for its unusual skin. *Saltasaurus* ('Salta Lizard'), named after the region of Argentina where it was found, was a giant plant-eater. It had many features in common with others of its kind, such as a long, flexible neck, pillar-like legs, and a slender tail. But, unlike other giant herbivores, *Saltasaurus* had armor-plated skin. Bony plates and nodules studded its back, giving it protection from the teeth and claws of predators. Huge plant-eaters may have survived in South America because they had evolved this form of self-defense.

● *The bony plates were oval and measured about 4 in (10 cm) across.*

● *The smaller nodules between the plates were pea-sized.*

Long neck

Armor-plated skin

Long, whip-like tail

Pillar-like legs

Saltasaurus *from:* Argentina, Uruguay.

Staurikosaurus *from:* Argentina, Brazil.

STAURIKOSAURUS *stor-ik-oh-sore-us*

Length: *7 ft (2 m)* **Weight:** *66 lb (30 kg)*

Lived: *225 million years ago (Late Triassic)*

A predatory meat-eater, *Staurikosaurus* ('Cross Lizard') is one of South America's first dinosaurs. It was named after the Southern Cross, a well-known group of stars visible in the skies of the southern hemisphere. *Staurikosaurus* lived at the same time as *Herrerasaurus*, another early carnivore from South America with which it has some features in common. Like *Herrerasaurus*, *Staurikosaurus* shows signs of being slightly primitive because some of its bones (particularly those in its legs and feet) were not as well developed as the ones that later carnivores had.

● *Its hands had five fingers and its feet had five toes. This feature identifies it as an early dinosaur, since later carnivores had three or four fingers and toes.*

Long tail

Short neck

Long legs

Dinosaurs in Europe

The study of dinosaurs began in Europe. As long ago as the 1600s it was known that fossilized bones found in quarries came from ancient animals. No one knew what the animals looked like, or how old they were. As more bones were found, scientists realized they came from creatures unlike any living animals. In 1822, an English scientist, James Parkinson, gave a name to one of these ancient animals. He called it *Megalosaurus* ('Great Lizard'), and it was the first dinosaur to be named. In 1842, Richard Owen, another Englishman, said that the animals belonged to a previously unknown group. He named the group 'Dinosauria', from the Greek words *deinos*, meaning 'terrible' and *sauros*, meaning 'lizard'.

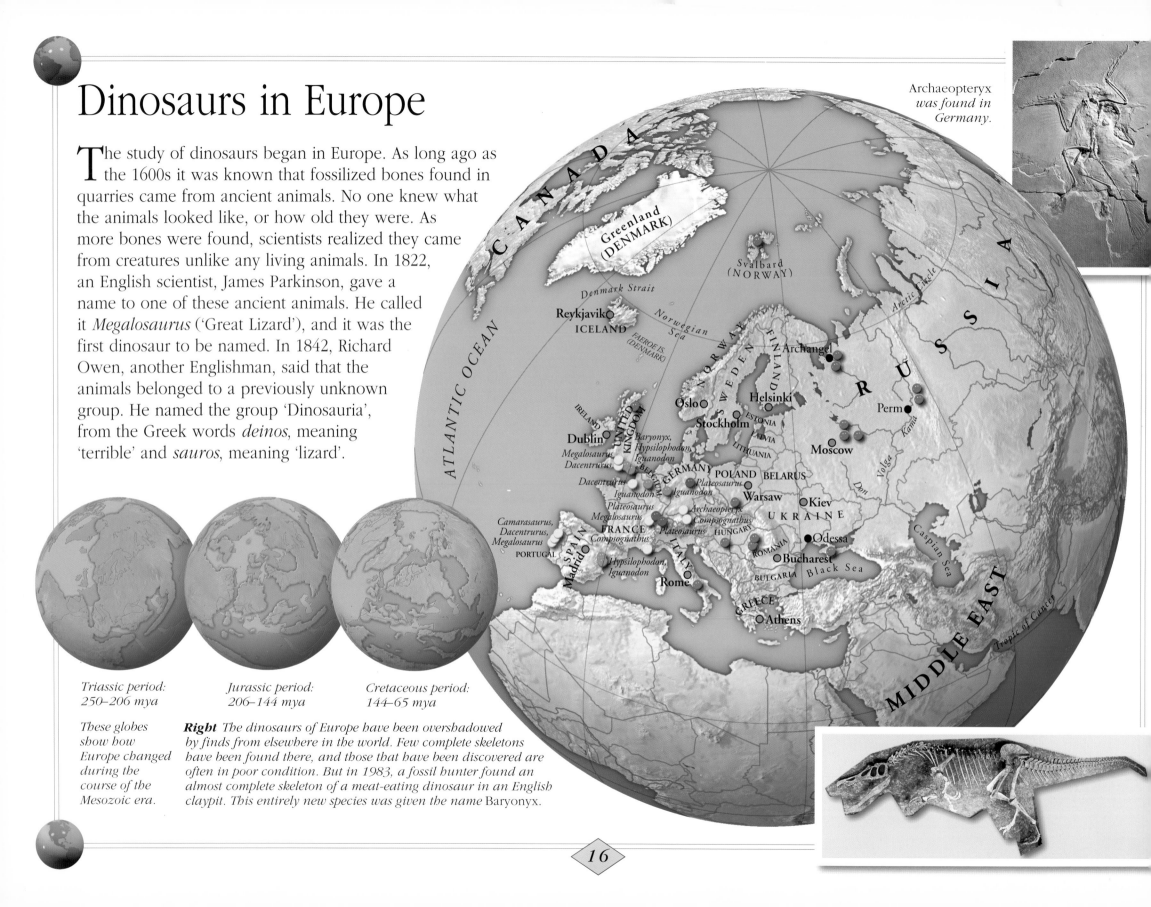

Archaeopteryx was found in Germany.

Triassic period: 250–206 mya

Jurassic period: 206–144 mya

Cretaceous period: 144–65 mya

These globes show how Europe changed during the course of the Mesozoic era.

Right *The dinosaurs of Europe have been overshadowed by finds from elsewhere in the world. Few complete skeletons have been found there, and those that have been discovered are often in poor condition. But in 1983, a fossil hunter found an almost complete skeleton of a meat-eating dinosaur in an English claypit. This entirely new species was given the name* Baryonyx.

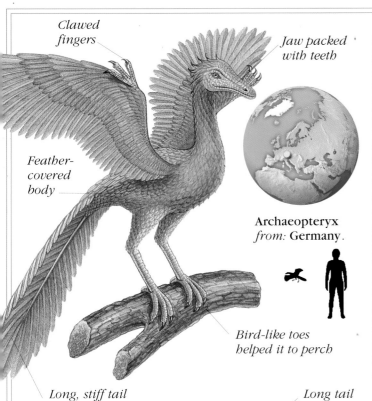

Clawed fingers

Jaw packed with teeth

Feather-covered body

Archaeopteryx *from: Germany.*

Long, stiff tail

Bird-like toes helped it to perch

ARCHAEOPTERYX *ar-key-op-ter-iks*

Length: *2 ft (60 cm)*	Weight: *6½lb (3 kg)*

Lived: *150 million years ago (Late Jurassic)*

One of the world's most remarkable ancient creatures flapped its primitive wings among the sparse Jurassic vegetation of Western Europe. This was *Archaeopteryx* ('Ancient Wing'), whose discovery in 1861 caused a major discussion among scientists which continues to this day. *Archaeopteryx* had feathers and a wishbone, two features associated with birds. But it also had features found in reptiles, such as teeth, a flexible neck, clawed fingers, long legs, and a long, bony tail. Fewer than 10 *Archaeopteryx* specimens have been found, all from a region in southern Germany. It is thought that *Archaeopteryx* is a link between dinosaurs and birds. It seems to be a stage in the origin of modern birds, a so-called 'dinobird'—not quite a true bird, but no longer a dinosaur either.

○ *Its wing muscles were weak, so it may have been unable to fly far. It may have used its wings to help it glide from tree to tree.*

○ *Its clawed fingers probably helped it to grip and climb trees.*

CAMARASAURUS *kam-are-ah-sore-us*

Length: *60 ft (18 m)*	Weight: *20 tons*

Lived: *150 million years ago (Late Jurassic)*

A well-known giant plant-eater from North America, *Camarasaurus* ('Chambered Lizard') has also been found in Europe. Its name comes from the fact that the bones in its spine were not solid. Instead, they had air spaces, or chambers, in them. These hollow backbones reduced the weight of the animal's skeleton, perhaps making it easier for the bulky *Camarasaurus* to move about. When looked at under a microscope, the teeth of an adult *Camarasaurus* appear scratched. This shows it probably ate coarse vegetation. Teeth from a young *Camarasaurus* are not scratched, which suggests it ate softer plants than its parents.

○ *Some scientists think that Camarasaurus could raise itself up on its back legs using its tail for support. If this is true, then maybe it did this to scare a predator away.*

○ *Camarasaurus walked on all fours. Its limbs were all about the same length.*

Long tail

Baryonyx *from: England.*

Camarasaurus *from: Portugal.*

BARYONYX *bar-ee-on-iks*

Length: *33 ft (10 m)*	Weight: *2 tons*

Lived: *125 million years ago (Early Cretaceous)*

It is the long curved thumb claws which gave *Baryonyx* ('Heavy Claw') its name. What makes this meat-eater from England notable is that the remains of its last meal were found within its stomach area. Fish scales from *Lepidotes* (a fish that grew to about 3 ft [1 m] in length, found inside *Baryonyx*'s rib-cage tell us something about its diet. Even without this tell-tale evidence other clues point to it being a fish-eater. For example, it had a long snout with a spoon-shaped tip, and its upper jaw was S-shaped in side view. Modern fish-eating crocodiles have jaws just like this. *Baryonyx* may have been a scavenger too, using its long snout to reach into the bodies and tug at the rotting flesh of animals that had been dead for some time.

○ *Each thumb claw was 14 in (35 cm) long.*

○ *Its jaws contained 96 small, sharp teeth. This is far more teeth than most other meat-eating dinosaurs had.*

○ *It had long front limbs and, unlike other meat-eaters, it may sometimes have walked on all fours.*

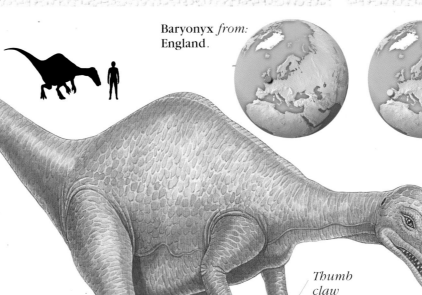

Long, narrow jaws

Thumb claw

Small, sharp teeth

Long front limbs

Heavy, thick-set legs

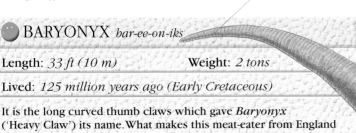

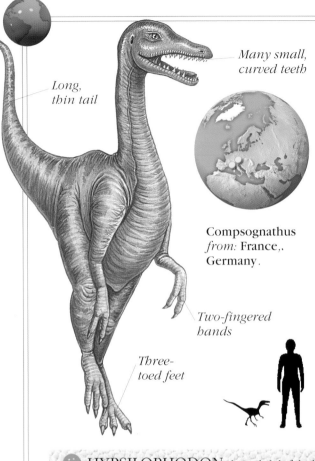

Long, thin tail

Many small, curved teeth

Compsognathus *from:* France, Germany.

Two-fingered hands

Three-toed feet

COMPSOGNATHUS *komp-so-nay-thus*

Length: *3 ft (1 m)*	Weight: *6½ lb (3 kg)*

Lived: *145 million years ago (Late Jurassic)*

A tiny dinosaur, about the size of a present-day turkey, *Compsognathus* ('Elegant Jaw') was a meat-eater that hunted small reptiles, mammals, and insects. It lived among wooded islands and lagoons. Within the rib-cage of one specimen the bones of a small lizard, *Bavarisaurus*, have been found, and it is this evidence that tells us something about the diet of *Compsognathus*. The presence of the lizard also tells us something else. Small lizards are fast-movers, never straying far from shelter. As *Compsognathus* was able to catch one, then it must have been an agile, speedy dinosaur. It must also have had good eyesight, able to see its victim amongst the rocks, ferns, and other hiding places.

○ *Compsognathus lived at the same time and in the same place as the first bird,* Archaeopteryx. *Because they were a similar size to each other, and had near-identical skeletons, it can be difficult to tell them apart.*

○ *Its small teeth were spaced apart, making them better for nipping at its victims rather than slicing into them, as the teeth of larger meat-eaters were designed to do.*

DACENTRURUS *day-sen-troo-rus*

Length: *16½ ft (5 m)*	Weight: *1 ton*

Lived: *155 million years ago (Late Jurassic)*

One of the few armored dinosaurs from Europe, little is known about *Dacentrurus* ('Pointed Tail'). It is named after the spikes on its tail. Pairs of spikes also grew on its back and neck. It is similar to a dinosaur from East Africa, *Kentrosaurus*. Dinosaurs like *Dacentrurus* and *Kentrosaurus*, whose bodies were protected by spikes and bony plates, are known as stegosaurs ('roof lizards'). These were large plant-eaters that walked slowly on all fours. Their body armor was for self-defense. If *Dacentrurus* was attacked, its spikes would have made it difficult for a predator to get close to it without injuring itself. And if *Dacentrurus* whipped its tail from side to side, it might have been able to drive a meat-eater away.

Pairs of spikes from neck to tail

○ Dacentrurus *was originally called 'Omosaurus' ('Shoulder Lizard') because it was thought spikes grew from its shoulders.*

HYPSILOPHODON *hip-sih-loh-foh-don*

Length: *7½ ft (2.3 m)*	Weight: *154 lb (70 kg)*

Lived: *120 million years ago (Early Cretaceous)*

A small, graceful dinosaur, the fossilized bones of many *Hypsilophodon* ('High-ridged Tooth') have been found together. This is taken as evidence that *Hypsilophodon* lived in herds rather than on its own. It was a plant-eater, nipping and tugging at soft vegetation with its horny beak. Inside its mouth were about 30 teeth, wide and sharp like chisel blades. As it grazed on leaves, horsetails, and palm fronds, it stuffed them into its cheek pouches. Then, as it chewed, its teeth chopped and crushed the vegetation until it was small enough to swallow. *Hypsilophodon* moved quickly on its two back legs—its arms and hands were probably used for grasping its food.

○ *As its teeth wore down and fell out, new ones grew in their place.*

○ *The long legs of* Hypsilophodon *indicate that it was a fast runner. With no other means of self-defense, speed was how it looked after itself. It could soon outrun a predator.*

Hypsilophodon *from:* England, Spain.

Horny beak

Grasping hands

Long, slender legs

Pillar-like heavy legs

Long, stiff tail

Dacentrurus *from:* England, France, Portugal.

● IGUANODON *ig-wa-no-don*

Length: *33 ft (10 m)*	Weight: *5 tons*

Lived: *130 million years ago (Early Cretaceous)*

Iguanodon ('Iguana Tooth') is one of the world's best-known dinosaurs, whose remains have been found in several parts of Western Europe, as well as in North America. A large herbivore, *Iguanodon* was a herd animal that grazed on low-growing vegetation, such as horsetails and ferns. At the front of its mouth was a bony, toothless beak that nipped off the soft, succulent parts of plants. Inside its mouth its tongue pushed food into its roomy cheek pouches, ready to be chewed to a digestible pulp by its sharp, serrated teeth. A notable feature of *Iguanodon* was a long, sharp spike that grew on each thumb. Perhaps this was how it defended itself in an attack, rearing up on its back legs and stabbing at its foe with its thumb spikes. Males may have used their thumb spikes in leadership contests.

● *In 1878, at Bernissart, Belgium, coal miners found a mass grave of about 30 Iguanodon. It is thought the animals had fallen down a deep ravine, or been caught by a flash flood.*

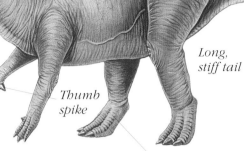

Long, stiff tail

Thumb spike

Wide, cow-like hoof

Iguanodon *from:* Belgium, England, Germany, Spain.

● MEGALOSAURUS *meg-al-oh-sore-us*

Length: *30 ft (9 m)*	Weight: *1 ton*

Lived: *170 million years ago (Middle Jurassic)*

The first dinosaur ever to be given a name (before the word 'dinosaur' had even been invented), *Megalosaurus* ('Great Lizard') was a powerful meat-eater. In spite of its important place in the history of dinosaur studies, *Megalosaurus* is not at all well known, because no complete specimen has yet been found. It is usually compared with other large carnivores, from which scientists imagine that it was both a hunter and a scavenger. One of its principal victims may have been *Iguanodon* which lived at the same time and in the same place as *Megalosaurus*.

● *Megalosaurus had long, curved teeth with serrated edges for slicing easily through skin and bone.*

● *A similar-looking dinosaur from North America, Torvosaurus ('Savage Lizard') is thought to be a close relative of Megalosaurus.*

Powerful legs with three toes

Megalosaurus *from:* England, France, Portugal.

● PLATEOSAURUS *plat-ee-oh-sore-us*

Length: *23 ft (7 m)*	Weight: *2 tons*

Lived: *220 million years ago (Late Triassic)*

A large four-legged herbivore, *Plateosaurus* ('Flat Lizard') is one of Europe's first giant dinosaurs. In common with other massive plant-eaters, *Plateosaurus* shares several features with them. It was long-necked and had a small head; its back legs were longer than its front limbs; its body was bulky, and it most probably carried stones in its stomach which crushed its food to a pulp for rapid digestion. With its long neck it could have reached up to high-growing leaves, which its leaf-shaped teeth would have stripped from their branches. Perhaps it also ate plants that grew on the ground. *Plateosaurus* finds are common in some parts of Europe, suggesting that this giant herbivore was one of the most abundant dinosaurs of its day.

● *Plateosaurus was probably a herd animal. At Trossingen, Germany, many have been found in a 'mass grave', suggesting that a herd was killed in a single accident, such as a flood.*

● *It is called 'Flat Lizard' because its teeth were flat-sided.*

● *It may have been able to rear up on its back legs to reach the very tops of tall trees.*

Tail vertebrae

Plateosaurus *from:* France, Germany, Switzerland.

Neck vertebrae

Small skull

Rib-cage

Five-fingered hands

Dinosaurs in Asia

Dinosaurs have been found across much of Asia. China and Mongolia are particularly rich in dinosaur fossils, and more than 100 different species of dinosaurs have been found here, which is more than anywhere else in the world. It is not only well-preserved skeletons that continue to be found in China and Mongolia—eggs and footprints are found here, too. Many great discoveries have been made in China, such as nesting sites of *Protoceratops* and *Oviraptor*. Feathered dinosaurs have also been found here, such as the remarkable *Caudipteryx*. The work of international expeditions in Asia is increasing the worldwide knowledge of dinosaurs. Asia also has some of the world's best dinosaur-only museums.

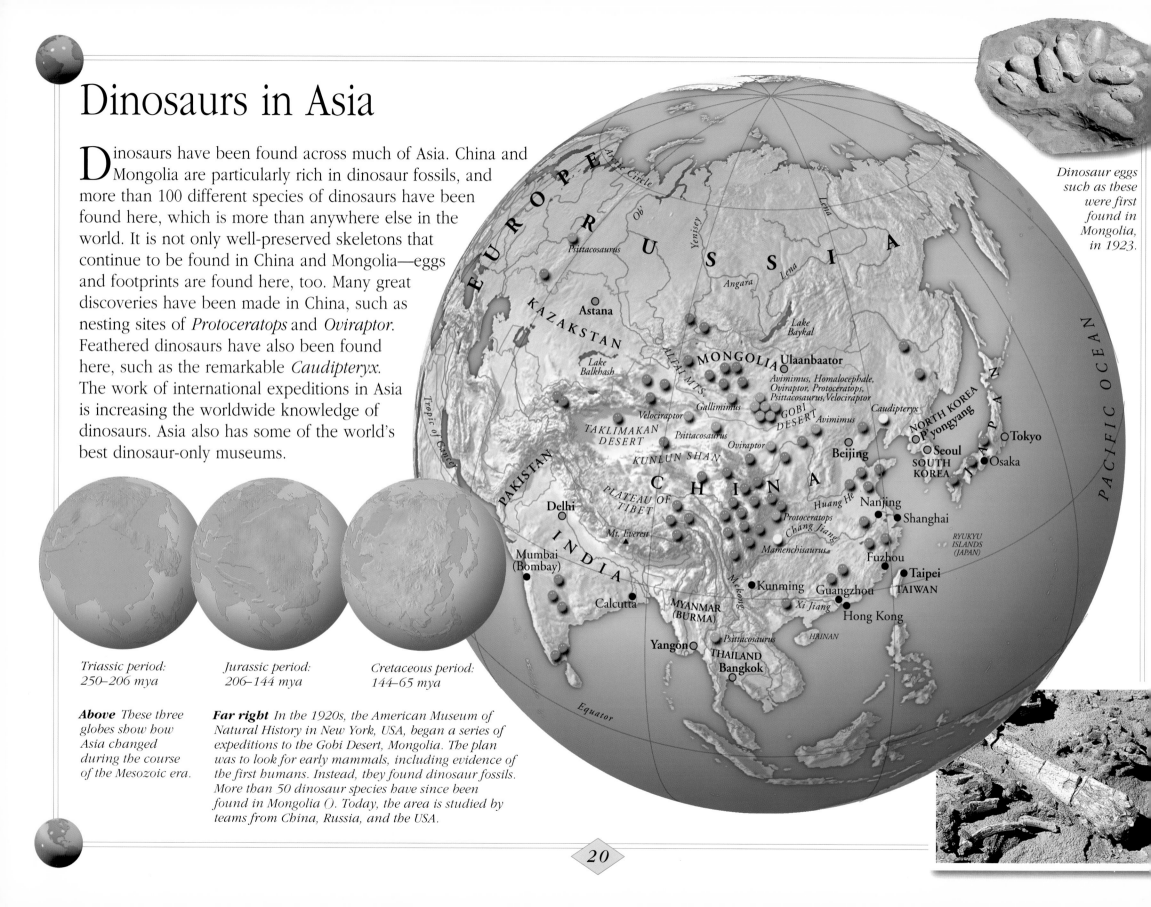

Dinosaur eggs such as these were first found in Mongolia, in 1923.

Triassic period: 250–206 mya

Jurassic period: 206–144 mya

Cretaceous period: 144–65 mya

Above *These three globes show how Asia changed during the course of the Mesozoic era.*

Far right *In the 1920s, the American Museum of Natural History in New York, USA, began a series of expeditions to the Gobi Desert, Mongolia. The plan was to look for early mammals, including evidence of the first humans. Instead, they found dinosaur fossils. More than 50 dinosaur species have since been found in Mongolia (). Today, the area is studied by teams from China, Russia, and the USA.*

AVIMIMUS *ay-vee-meem-us*

Length: *5 ft (1.5 m)*   **Weight:** *33 lb (15 kg)*

Lived: *80 million years ago (Late Cretaceous)*

The bird-like appearance of *Avimimus* ('Bird Mimic') is its most striking feature. But *Avimimus* was not a bird. It was a long-legged dinosaur that had some of the features we can see in birds. For example, its head was particularly bird-like, having large eyes, a toothless beak, and a large brain. Its arms also show bird-like qualities, particularly in the way it could fold them in toward its body, just like a bird folds its wings. Although no evidence has yet been found for feathers on *Avimimus*, Russian scientists who have studied it believe it may have been one of the first feathered dinosaurs. They think it grew feathers on its arms. If this is true, then when *Avimimus* stretched its arms, they would have looked like little wings.

○ Avimimus *could not fly. Its arms were much too short for any kind of flight.*

○ Avimimus *was probably an omnivore, a creature that has a diet of both plants and meat. It may have fed mainly on insects.*

Teeth only at the front of the upper jaw

Short arms

Fan-like tail feathers

Caudipteryx *from:* China.

CAUDIPTERYX *cor-dip-ter-iks*

Length: *3 ft (1 m)*   **Weight:** *6½ lb (3 kg)*

Lived: *130 million years ago (Late Jurassic)*

Caudipteryx ('Tail Feather') was a feathered dinosaur, first found in China in the 1990s. When scientists from China and Canada studied it they thought it was an *Archaeopteryx*, or a close relative. However, as the fossil was cleaned and examined in great detail, they became aware that the animal was different from *Archaeopteryx*. In particular, its teeth were different. It was a new species of dinosaur—one of the so-called 'dinobirds'—and it was named *Caudipteryx* after its eye-catching long tail feathers. Perhaps *Caudipteryx* fanned its tail feathers in courtship displays, when it was looking for a mate, as birds do today. These feathers could also have been used to improve the dinosaur's speed and balance as it ran.

○ Caudipteryx *could not fly. Its arms were too short to act as wings, and, more importantly, its 'flight' feathers were not the correct shape to get it airborne. True flight feathers (like those in birds) are slightly curved and uneven, whereas the ones that* Caudipteryx *had were straight and evenly shaped.*

○ *Small stones inside its stomach crushed its food to a digestible pulp.*

Body may have had feathers

Bird-like head

Stiff, bony tail

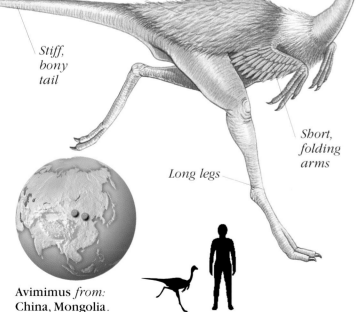

Short, folding arms

Long legs

Avimimus *from:* China, Mongolia.

GALLIMIMUS *gal-ee-meem-us*

Length: *20 ft (6 m)*   **Weight:** *1,100 lb (500 kg)*

Lived: *75 million years ago (Late Cretaceous)*

Gallimimus ('Chicken Mimic') was the largest of a group of dinosaurs called ornithomimids ('ostrich dinosaurs'). It was a speedy, two-legged animal that lived on a mixed diet of plants, insects, and small animals. Like other members of its group it had a bird-like, toothless beak, and large eyes. With its head held high in the air it was probably able to see for long distances. Its long neck would have come in useful when it poked around in undergrowth for food, and its strong clawed fingers were the ideal tools for scratching around on the ground.

Long, stiff tail

○ Gallimimus *could probably run at great speed. A modern ostrich can run at up to 43 mph (70 km/h), a speed which it is thought* Gallimimus *could easily equal.*

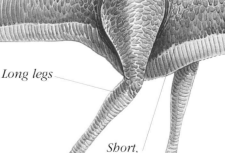

Gallimimus *from:* Mongolia

Long, flexible neck

Long legs

Three clawed toes

Short, compact body

Grasping hand

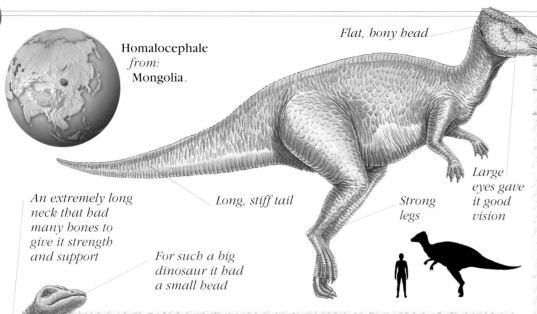

Homalocephale
from:
Mongolia.

Flat, bony head

Long, stiff tail

Strong legs

Large eyes gave it good vision

An extremely long neck that had many bones to give it strength and support

For such a big dinosaur it had a small head

HOMALOCEPHALE *hom-al-oh-seff-ah-lee*

Length: *10 ft (3 m)*   **Weight:** *95 lb (43 kg)*

Lived: *80 million years ago (Late Cretaceous)*

Homalocephale ('Even Head') belonged to a group of dinosaurs called pachycephalosaurids ('bone-headed'). These were small- to medium-sized plant-eaters with heavy bodies. Their distinctive feature was an exceptionally thick-boned skull, from which protruded bony knobs and short spikes. Unlike most other 'boneheads', whose skulls were dome-shaped, *Homalocephale* had a flat, even-shaped skull, hence its name. There were

bony nodules, ridges and short spikes on the top and back of its skull, and also on its cheeks. This dinosaur had large eyes, and scientists believe it also had a good sense of smell. Both these factors would have been of great use to *Homalocephale*, since it had no means of self-defense other than being able to run from danger. With good eyesight and smell it could detect an approaching predator.

- Like other 'boneheads', such as Stegoceras from North America, Homalocephale *may have used its bony head in pushing contests to determine who should be a group leader.*

- *It walked on all fours.*

- *It lived in a dry, desert-like environment and may have moved in herds.*

- Homalocephale *was a browser that mostly ate leaves.*

MAMENCHISAURUS *mah-men-chee-sore-us*

Length: *82 ft (25 m)*   **Weight:** *27 tons*

Lived: *160 million years ago (Late Jurassic)*

A huge, long-necked herbivore, *Mamenchisaurus* ('Mamen Brook Lizard') is one of the largest of all Chinese dinosaurs. It was discovered in the 1950s, at a site in central China where so-called 'dragon's bones' had been found over many years. When the bones of *Mamenchisaurus* were reassembled, the full size of this giant was

revealed. It had one of the longest necks of all dinosaurs, measuring some 46 ft (14 m) in length. Why it needed such a long neck is still something of a puzzle, but scientists usually say it was to help it stretch up to leaves that grew at the top of tall trees. One thing is clear, it must have had a powerful heart that could pump blood around its massive body.

- *'Dragon's bones' found in China may not have come from dinosaurs. Some scientists think they are bones from ancient mammals, not reptiles.*

- Mamenchisaurus *had spoon-shaped teeth which were ideal for combing through vegetation, stripping leaves from their branches.*

Oviraptor
from:
China,
Mongolia.

OVIRAPTOR *oh-vee-rap-tor*

Length: *6 ft (1.8 m)*   **Weight:** *44 lb (20 kg)*

Lived: *80 million years ago (Late Cretaceous)*

When this bird-like dinosaur was discovered in the 1920s, it was found on top of a nest of eggs. At that time the eggs were thought to belong to *Protoceratops*. Because scientists thought the new dinosaur was stealing eggs from the nest of a *Protoceratops*, they named it *Oviraptor* ('Egg Thief')—but this idea is now known to be wrong. Far from stealing eggs, *Oviraptor* had been found lying on its own eggs, no doubt incubating them until they hatched. Long legs gave *Oviraptor* the power of speed, and strong, clawed hands helped it grasp its prey. Its toothless beak was moved by powerful muscles, and on top of its head grew a tall, bony crest. The purpose of the crest is unclear.

Crest

- Oviraptor *was a hunter, running down smaller animals which it killed with kicks and bites.*

Toothless beak

Front legs were shorter than its back legs

Mamenchisaurus
from: China.

PROTOCERATOPS pro-toe-ser-a-tops

Length: 6 ft (1.8 m) **Weight:** 400 lb (180 kg)

Lived: 80 million years ago (Late Cretaceous)

A squat herbivore, *Protoceratops* ('First Horned Face') has provided scientists with a wealth of valuable information. It was found in the Gobi Desert, Mongolia, in the 1920s. The find spot turned out to be a nesting site where adults, juveniles, hatchlings, eggs and nests were found. It was a major discovery because these were the first dinosaur eggs ever to be found. With only short legs (it was no taller than 2 ft [60 cm]), *Protoceratops* was a slow mover, but what it lacked in speed it made up for with a heavily protected large-sized head. A wide frill of bone grew from the back of its skull, protecting the soft skin of its neck. Its snout ended in a powerful parrot-like beak which could as easily bite through twigs as it could through the arm or leg of a small predator out to attack it. Behind its beak were small teeth which chewed on food until ready to swallow.

● *Protoceratops laid its eggs in a spiral pattern inside its nest, which was a shallow hole scooped in the sand of its desert home. Eggs were like cylinders, 8 in (20 cm) long and 7 in (17.5 cm) around the middle.*

● *A newly hatched* Protoceratops *was 12 in (30 cm) long. The young probably stayed close to their parents for several years, until they were strong enough to lead their own independent lives.*

Bony neck frill

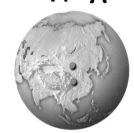

Back legs were longer than front legs

Strong, parrot-like beak

Protoceratops *from:* China, Mongolia.

Psittacosaurus *from:* China, Mongolia, Russia, Thailand.

Box-like head with powerful beak

PSITTACOSAURUS sit-ak-oh-sore-us

Length: 6½ ft (2 m) **Weight:** 176 lb (80 kg)

Lived: 110 million years ago (Early Cretaceous)

Psittacosaurus ('Parrot Lizard', after the parrot-like shape of its beak) was a small, lightly built, two-legged herbivore. It was one of the first dinosaurs to develop a distinctive beak, which it used in a slicing motion to chop through tough vegetation. Once inside its mouth, food was pushed into its cheek pouches by its strong tongue. After the leaves, palm fronds and other plant material had been crushed by its teeth, the pulp was gulped down into its stomach, to be further broken down by the grinding action of stones, bacteria and digestive juices.

● *Psittacosaurus was an early member of the ceratopsid ('horned face') group of dinosaurs. Its cheek bones were prominent, and it is possible that over millions of years they became the horns of dinosaurs such as* Triceratops.

● *A newly hatched* Psittacosaurus *was tiny—the size of a robin.*

Long arms with grasping hands

Long legs

VELOCIRAPTOR vel-o-see-rap-tor

Length: 6 ft (1.8 m) **Weight:** 55 lb (25 kg)

Lived: 70 million years ago (Late Cretaceous)

A fast-moving meat-eating dinosaur, *Velociraptor* ('Quick Predator') was one of the supreme hunters of its day. Similar to *Deinonychus* from North America, it too had a large sickle-like claw on the second toe of each foot. Inside its long jaws were sharp, serrated teeth—the perfect shape for slicing meat. A lot is known about how and what it fought, since a *Velociraptor* has been found in Mongolia locked in battle with a *Protoceratops*. The right arm of the *Velociraptor* is gripped in the beak of the *Protoceratops*, while the *Velociraptor* seems to be clawing at the neck of its prey. It was probably kicking the *Protoceratops*, trying to rip its hide with its claws. *Velociraptor* was probably a pack animal, preying on old and weak animals.

● *Velociraptor had a large head and a big brain. It probably had a high degree of intelligence.*

● *Some scientists believe that small meat-eaters like* Velociraptor *had feathers. This is yet to be proved.*

Tail held straight behind for balance as it moved at speed

Long sharp claw held off the ground when it moved

Strong arms

Velociraptor *from:* China, Mongolia.

23

Dinosaurs in Africa

Dinosaurs lived in Africa throughout the Mesozoic era, and many fossil sites have been found there. Some of the first African dinosaurs were unearthed on the island of Madagascar in the 1890s. One hundred years later, in 1999, the world's oldest-known dinosaur was found there. This yet-to-be-named herbivore is at least 230 million years old. Elsewhere, the countries of North Africa, particularly Morocco, have produced many dinosaur fossils, such as the sail-backed *Spinosaurus*. From East Africa a site in Tanzania has produced the bones of hundreds of dinosaurs. Southern Africa is known for *Lesothosaurus*. So far, little scientific work has been done in West Africa.

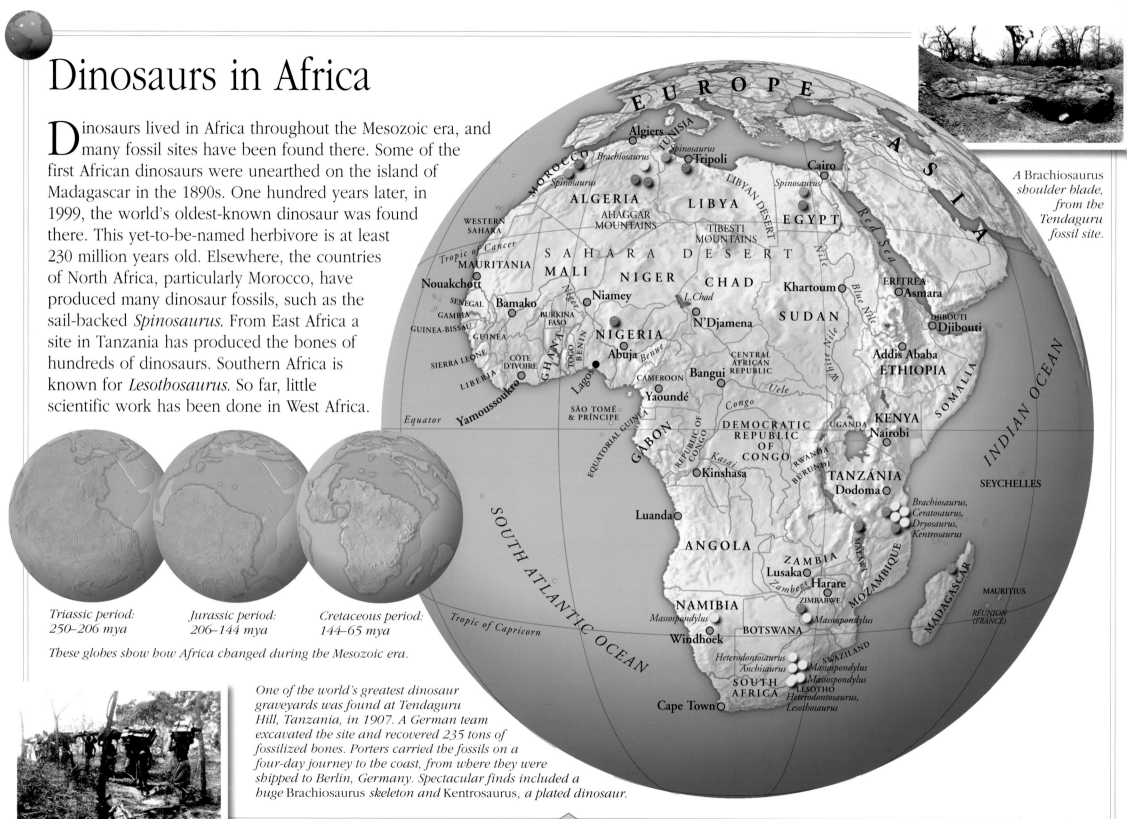

A Brachiosaurus shoulder blade, from the Tendaguru fossil site.

Triassic period: 250–206 mya

Jurassic period: 206–144 mya

Cretaceous period: 144–65 mya

These globes show how Africa changed during the Mesozoic era.

One of the world's greatest dinosaur graveyards was found at Tendaguru Hill, Tanzania, in 1907. A German team excavated the site and recovered 235 tons of fossilized bones. Porters carried the fossils on a four-day journey to the coast, from where they were shipped to Berlin, Germany. Spectacular finds included a huge Brachiosaurus *skeleton and* Kentrosaurus, *a plated dinosaur.*

ANCHISAURUS *an-key-sore-us*

Length: *8 ft (2.4 m)* | **Weight:** *60 lb (27 kg)*

Lived: *190 million years ago (Early Jurassic)*

This small dinosaur was given the name *Anchisaurus* ('Near Lizard') because its body was close to the ground. It was an early species of plant-eating dinosaur, and was an ancestor of the giant herbivores that lived later, such as *Brachiosaurus*. *Anchisaurus* was able to walk on its two back legs as well as on all fours. When feeding, it could rear up on its back legs, supporting its body by resting its tail on the ground. In this way it could reach leaves that grew high up. It also ate plants that grew on the ground. Its weak teeth nipped at soft, easy-to-chew plants.

◯ *Anchisaurus also lived in North America. Its fossilized bones were found in northeast USA in 1818. It was the first dinosaur discovered in North America.*

Anchisaurus *from:* South Africa.

Long tail held off the ground

Large nostrils on top of head

Small head

Blunt, shaped teeth

Five fingers on each hand

Four toes on each foot

Brachiosaurus *from:* Algeria, Tanzania.

BRACHIOSAURUS *brak-ee-oh-sore-us*

Length: *82 ft (25 m)* | **Weight:** *30–50 tons*

Lived: *150 million years ago (Late Jurassic)*

A giant herbivore, *Brachiosaurus* ('Arm Lizard') is named after its long front legs. Scientists who studied it in the early 1900s noticed how they grew from its shoulders, as if they were arms. In spite of its name, *Brachiosaurus* was a four-legged dinosaur that walked slowly along, perhaps at no more than 2 mph (3 km/h). It may have lived in herds, feeding on low-growing ferns and cycads, and the tough needle-like leaves of conifer trees. With such a huge body to feed, *Brachiosaurus* would have needed a large amount of food—one estimate puts its daily food intake at 440 lb (200 kg) of plants every day. For a creature so big, *Brachiosaurus* had a small head and a tiny brain. Its weak jaws held 52 chisel-like teeth. To eat, *Brachiosaurus* probably combed its teeth back and forth through plants, stripping leaves from their branches.

◯ *It is still a mystery why* Brachiosaurus *had nostrils on top of its head. They were large, which suggests a good sense of smell. Perhaps it was better at finding food by smell, rather than sight.*

Its neck was 30 ft (9 m) long

Long, stiff tail

Front legs longer than back legs

Nose horn

CERATOSAURUS *ser-a-toe-sore-us*

Length: *20 ft (6 m)* | **Weight:** *1 ton*

Lived: *150 million years ago (Late Jurassic)*

A fast-moving meat-eater, *Ceratosaurus* ('Horned Lizard') earned its name from the short horn that grew on the tip of its snout. Horny ridges also grew near its eyes. Given that its main weapon of attack was its long, dagger-like teeth, its head protrusions must have had another purpose. Males may have used them for display purposes, such as when they attracted mates. The horns on females may have been smaller than those on males. *Ceratosaurus* was probably a lone predator, like other large carnivores. It would have preyed on smaller animals, grasping them with its clawed hands then kicking and biting them.

◯ Ceratosaurus *had a large head. When it ate, the bones of its skull moved sideways, letting it gulp down large chunks of meat.*

◯ *When its teeth fell out—either through age, disease or damage—*Ceratosaurus *was able to grow new ones to replace them.*

Curved claws

Walked on back legs

Ceratosaurus *from:* Tanzania.

DRYOSAURUS *dry-oh-sore-us*

Length: *13 ft (4 m)*   **Weight:** *170 lb (77 kg)*

Lived: *150 million years ago (Late Jurassic)*

An agile herbivore, *Dryosaurus* ('Oak Lizard') is characterized by a horny beak and high-crowned cheek teeth. There were no teeth at the front of its beak. When it ate, its beak cut through vegetation, which was then pushed into its cheek pouches by its strong tongue. Long teeth, patterned with deep ridges, then began to grind the plants, quickly reducing them to a pulp which was easy to swallow.

There were five fingers on each of its hands, and it probably used them to hold and pull at vegetation. If threatened by an attacker, *Dryosaurus* had no means of fighting back. Instead, it defended itself by fleeing from the danger. Its leg bones were hollow, which reduced its overall weight. With less body weight to carry, *Dryosaurus* could out-run its enemy.

○ Dryosaurus *was one of the dinosaurs found at the world-famous fossil site at Tendaguru, Tanzania. It is also known from North America.*

○ *It is thought to have lived in herds, traveling long distances over land as it moved from one grazing site to another.*

Kentrosaurus *from:* Tanzania.

Hip spine

Tail spines, in pairs

Back legs were twice as long as front legs

Two rows of bony plates

Small head

Some teeth were short tusks, like the canines of a dog

Dryosaurus ran at speed on its long back legs

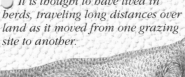

Dryosaurus *from:* Tanzania.

Strong, grasping arms and hands

Long, stiff tail

Clawed toes

KENTROSAURUS *ken-troh-sore-us*

Length: *16 ft (5 m)*   **Weight:** *1 ton*

Lived: *155 million years ago (Late Jurassic)*

Kentrosaurus ('Spiked Lizard') was a stegosaur. Dinosaurs of this group were characterized by bony spikes and plates (called scutes) which protected their bodies. Like all other stegosaurs, *Kentrosaurus* was a heavy, slow-moving plant-eater. It lived in herds, grazing on low-growing plants which grew close to rivers. The long spikes and flat plates that covered its neck, back, and tail were for self-defense. Being large and slow, *Kentrosaurus* was an easy target for a predator—but no doubt it had its own methods for seeing off an attacker. For example, it could use its tail like a whip, lashing out at a predator with its lethal spikes. An attack from the side might also have been difficult, since long spikes grew out from its hips, and maybe from its shoulders, too.

○ Kentrosaurus *was about half the size of the best-known stegosaur, the North American* Stegosaurus. *It was about 3 ft (1m) tall at the hips.*

HETERODONTOSAURUS *het-er-oh-dont-oh-sore-us*

Length: *4 ft (1.2 m)*   **Weight:** *5½ lb (2.5 kg)*

Lived: *205 million years ago (Early Jurassic)*

This dinosaur is named after its unusual teeth. *Heterodontosaurus* ('Different-toothed Lizard') had three types of teeth—most dinosaurs only had one type. At the front of its lower jaw was a horny beak which made contact with a bony pad on the upper jaw. Either side of the bony pad were small, sharp teeth, then tusk-like teeth. At the back of its mouth

were close-packed chewing teeth. A small herbivore, *Heterodontosaurus* grazed on low-growing plants, nipping them off with its beak and front teeth. It may have used its tusks to puncture and rip through tough plants. These special teeth may have had a more important function—males may have used them in a mating display.

○ *It is thought that only males grew the tusk-like teeth. A* Heterodontosaurus *skull has been found that does not have these teeth, and this may have belonged to a female.*

○ Heterodontosaurus *was a lightly built dinosaur, able to run at speed on its two long back legs. It had long shins and feet, which mark it out as a running animal.*

Heterodontosaurus *from:* South Africa, Lesotho.

LESOTHOSAURUS *le-soo-too-sore-us*

Length: *3 ft (1 m)*	Weight: *66 lb (30 kg)*

Lived: *200 million years ago (Early Jurassic)*

Living in herds that scampered quickly across the hot, semi-desert plains of what is today Lesotho and South Africa, this small dinosaur was built for speed. Named after the country in which it was first found, *Lesothosaurus* ('Lesotho Lizard') was a lightly built animal. Its leg bones were hollow, an important weight-saving feature designed to help it run fast. *Lesothosaurus* was a herbivore that ate low-growing plants. Its small teeth were sharp, and shaped like arrowheads. As it chewed its food its upper and lower teeth interlocked. Over time they wore down and fell out, and new ones grew in their place. *Lesothosaurus* may have dug burrows, like some small lizards do today. Two *Lesothosaurus* have been found curled up together, as if they were sleeping inside a burrow, as if they were sleeping inside a burrow. A burrow would have a been a safe place to rest, and hide from predators.

⬤ If Lesothosaurus *turns out to be the same dinosaur as* Fabrosaurus, *it will have to be called by this other name.*

⬤ Some people think Lesothosaurus *may have had a mixed diet, eating meat from insects and carrion as well as plants. It is thought to have lived in herds,*

Long legs with four toes on each foot

Small head, large eyes

Short arms with five fingers on each hand

Lesothosaurus *from:* Lesotho.

Small head

Long neck

Massospondylus *from:* Lesotho, Namibia. South Africa, Zimbabwe.

MASSOSPONDYLUS *mas-oh-spon-die-lus*

Length: *16½ ft (5 m)*	Weight: *1 ton*

Lived: *200 million years ago (Early Jurassic)*

Massospondylus ('Massive Vertebrae') is an early example of a long-necked long-tailed herbivore. In spite of its length, it was not very tall, perhaps measuring little more than 3 ft (1 m) at the hips. It was only toward the end of the Jurassic that the truly gigantic herbivores appeared, such as *Apatosaurus* and *Brachiosaurus*. But even in the early Jurassic period, *Massospondylus* was showing signs of what was to come later. Its bulky body was supported on four sturdy legs, its tail was stiff, and its teeth seem suited to stripping leaves from branches. Stomach stones show that its food was crushed to aid its digestion. The stones found in a specimen from Zimbabwe came from a place 12½ miles (20 km) from where the animal's fossil was found. It may have lived in herds that traveled long distances.

⬤ Massospondylus *was named in 1854 by Richard Owen, the creator of the word 'dinosaur'.*

⬤ *This dinosaur has also been found in Arizona, USA.*

Long, stiff tail

SPINOSAURUS *spy-no-sore-us*

Length: *49 ft (15 m)*	Weight: *4 tons*

Lived: *100 million years ago (Middle Cretaceous)*

A huge carnivore, *Spinosaurus* ('Spine Lizard') is named after the row of long bony spines which grew from its backbone. These spines were up to 6½ ft (2 m) long, and their purpose was to support a fan-like skin 'fin' which ran the length of its back. Fossils of this strange-looking dinosaur have only ever been found in North Africa. The fin may have been brightly colored and used for display purposes, acting as a calling sign to others of its species. It may also have been used to scare off predators, especially if *Spinosaurus* could change it to a warning colour by flushing it red with blood. Another theory is that it acted as a heat regulator, trapping heat on cool days and releasing heat on hot days. In this way *Spinosaurus* could control its body temperature.

⬤ Spinosaurus *had straight teeth, not curved teeth like other carnivores. It may have eaten fish and land animals.*

Spinosaurus *from:* Egypt, Morocco, Tunisia.

Skin fin supported by bone spines

Teeth and jaw shape, like those of Baryonyx *from Europe, seem adapted for a diet of fish*

Dinosaurs in Australia and New Zealand

Triassic period
250–206 mya

Jurassic period
206–144 mya

Cretaceous period
144–65 mya

Very few dinosaurs have been found in Australia. It is the flattest of all the continents, and for much of the Mesozoic era a large part of it lay under the sea. Dinosaur fossils that are found here tend to come from the eastern part of the continent, where there are fossil-bearing rocky outcrops. Although few dinosaur bones have been found in Australia, many trackways have been discovered. These footprints belong to both large and small dinosaurs, which is strong evidence that Australia was indeed home to many different dinosaur species. *Minmi*, a small armored dinosaur, and *Muttaburrasaurus*, which resembled *Iguanodon*, are two of the continent's better-known dinosaurs.

New Zealand has fewer known dinosaur species than Australia, and none have yet been named. They resemble the dinosaurs of Antarctica. Both New Zealand and Australia were once joined to Antarctica until they broke away about 40 million years ago.

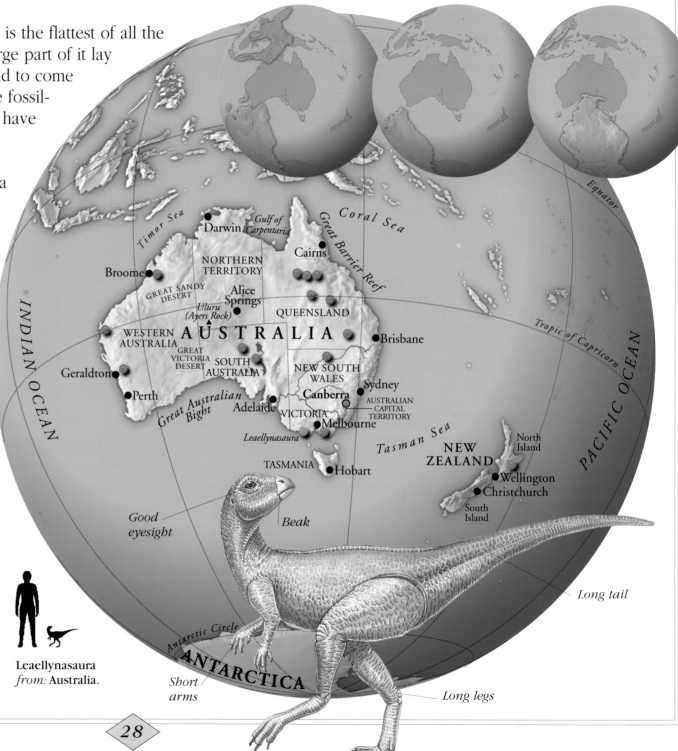

Leaellynasaura *from:* **Australia.**

Good eyesight

Beak

Short arms

Long tail

Long legs

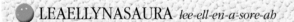

● LEAELLYNASAURA *lee-ell-en-a-sore-ah*

Length: *3 ft (1 m)*	Weight: *44 lb (20 kg)*

Lived: *105 million years ago (Early Cretaceous)*

Discovered at Dinosaur Cove, a fossil site in Victoria, southeast Australia, *Leaellynasaura* ('Leaellyn's Lizard') was a small, two-legged herbivore. It had similar features to other members of its group (*Leaellynasaura* was a hypsilophodontid), such as a horny beak and high-crowned cheek teeth. It may have been able to see in poor light, since it lived at a time when Australia was further south than it is today. Winters would have been longer, and daylight hours shorter. *Leaellynasaura* may have been specially adapted to these conditions.

● *The rock at Dinosaur Cove in which the bones of* Leaellynasaura *and other dinosaurs were found was so hard that gelignite was used to break it open.*

ANKYLOSAUR an-kee-loh-sore

Length: *33 ft (10 m)*   **Weight:** *5 tons*

Lived: *70 million years ago (Late Cretaceous)*

Ankylosaurs ('fused-together lizards') were a widespread family of armor-plated dinosaurs. They lived towards the end of the Mesozoic era and are known from North America, Asia, and Australia. In 1986, the skull and some bony plates from an ankylosaur were found on James Ross Island, just off the coast of the frozen continent of Antarctica. It was the first dinosaur to be found on this continent. Although it has not been linked to any particular kind of ankylosaur (and so does not have a species name), it is clear that it had many features in common with other members of its group. It was a four-legged herbivore whose body was protected by bony plates and nodules.

● *This unnamed ankylosaur was not alone on Antarctica. Remains of other plant-eaters and also meat-eaters have been found there.*

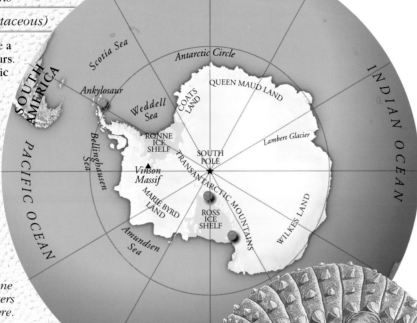

Unnamed ankylosaur from: Antarctica.

Long head with large eyes

Troodon *from:* **Canada, Russia, USA** *(Alaska, Montana, Wyoming).*

Long arms with long clawed fingers on its hands

Slender, long legs

TROODON troo-oh-don

Length: *7 ft (2 m)*   **Weight:** *88 lb (40 kg)*

Lived: *70 million years ago (Late Cretaceous)*

An eagle-eyed carnivore, *Troodon* ('Wounding Tooth') is known from sites below the northern polar circle in Canada and the USA. But it also lived within the polar region and has been found in Alaska, USA, and also in Russia. It was a sleek dinosaur, able to move at great speed to chase its prey, such as smaller reptiles and mammals. Its eyes were large, about 2 in (50 mm) across, which suggests it had a good sense of vision. Some scientists believe it may have been a night hunter, able to detect its prey in the dark. For those that ventured to the far north, good vision would have been essential in the region's poor light.

● *In Montana, USA, Troodon teeth have been found among the nests of plant-eaters, suggesting it ate eggs.*

● *Troodon was named in 1856 on the evidence of one tooth. Troodon bones were not found until the 1980s.*

Dinosaurs in the polar regions

It seems odd to think of dinosaurs living in the polar regions—places with low temperatures and little daylight. Since the mid-1980s, fossils and footprints have been found in both areas, showing that dinosaurs did live within the polar regions.

Dinosaurs of the northern polar region include *Albertosaurus* from Alaska, USA, and *Stegosaurus* from Russia. *Troodon* has been found in Alaska and Russia. Dinosaurs of the southern polar region have been found in Antarctica. Those from Australia and New Zealand are also polar dinosaurs, since these lands were once joined to Antarctica.

Death of the dinosaurs

There are almost 100 different theories about why dinosaurs died out. Some theories are silly (aliens hunted them), some cannot be proved (a plague killed them all), and some are worth taking seriously.

One idea popular with scientists is the impact theory. This states that a giant meteorite (a space rock) slammed into the Earth about 65 million years ago. The impact sent a huge volume of dust into the atmosphere, and it was blown around the globe. The dust stopped sunlight from reaching the ground and a period of darkness began. Plants died through lack of sunlight and, with nothing to eat, plant-eating dinosaurs starved to death. The meat-eaters then died as their food supplies disappeared.

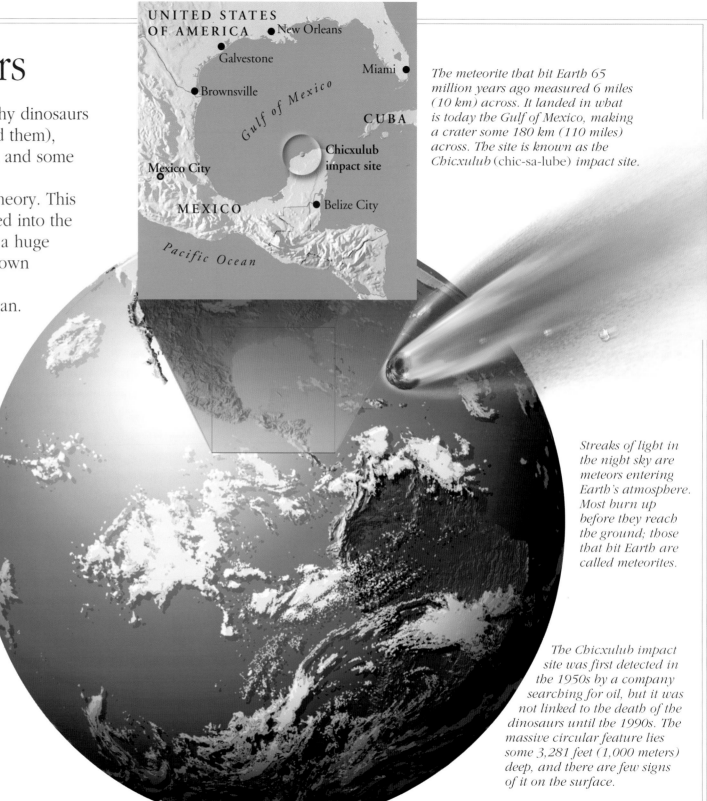

The meteorite that hit Earth 65 million years ago measured 6 miles (10 km) across. It landed in what is today the Gulf of Mexico, making a crater some 180 km (110 miles) across. The site is known as the Chicxulub (chic-sa-lube) impact site.

UNITED STATES OF AMERICA
● New Orleans
● Galvestone
Miami ●
● Brownsville
Gulf of Mexico
CUBA
Chicxulub impact site
Mexico City
○
● Belize City
MEXICO
Pacific Ocean

Streaks of light in the night sky are meteors entering Earth's atmosphere. Most burn up before they reach the ground; those that hit Earth are called meteorites.

The Chicxulub impact site was first detected in the 1950s by a company searching for oil, but it was not linked to the death of the dinosaurs until the 1990s. The massive circular feature lies some 3,281 feet (1,000 meters) deep, and there are few signs of it on the surface.

Another theory states that dinosaurs died out because of volcanic eruptions. In this theory scientists say that volcanoes, erupting over thousands of years, pumped ash and carbon dioxide gas into the atmosphere. The climate changed (it either grew hotter or colder, no one is certain), and dinosaurs died because they could not adapt.

Discovering dinosaurs

Collectors have been fascinated by fossils for hundreds of years, but it is only within the past two centuries that they've aroused the serious interest of scientists. Today, teams of paleontologists (the scientists who study dinosaurs and other ancient animals) go on expeditions to the places where they know they will find dinosaur remains. Because the continents have changed their shapes so much, both during the time the dinosaurs were alive and since, their fossils are only found in certain parts of the world. Once found, it takes a lot of effort to carefully excavate the fossils, pack them, and then transport them to a museum where they are prepared for display and study.

Bone being coated in plastered bandage.

Fossils packed in crates

Brushing removes dust

Fossil hunters know what to look for. A bone weathering from a cliff or a curiously shaped stone may be the clues to a dinosaur fossil nearby. Fossils are freed from the ground with hammers and chisels. It's slow work and great care is taken not to damage the remains.

The bones are made ready to transport to the museum. Each bone is coated in a thick layer of plaster-coated bandage. When the plaster has set hard, the bone is carefully lifted and packed into crates.

As more of the dinosaur is exposed, the bones are cleaned, drawn and photographed. Every bone is given a number so that scientists will know how to rebuild the skeleton when it is in the museum.

In the museum, the bones from the excavation are taken to the conservation department. There, the plaster jackets are removed. To make the bones strong enough to handle, cracks are repaired and missing pieces are filled in. Eventually, the skeleton is mounted on a metal frame, called an armature, and it goes on display. If the skeleton is not complete, the bones are kept in boxes in the museum's storeroom.

A fully mounted dinosaur skeleton like this Apatosaurus is an impressive sight. But even though many scientists have worked hard to create such a restoration, years of work still lie ahead. Scientific articles will be written about the fossil, and details about the animal's lifestyle will be worked out. It might have died millions of years ago, but its bones have a story to tell.

Index

Picture credits

Maps:
Mountain High Maps
© Digital Wisdom.

Illustrations:
JB Illustrations (Julian Baker, Janet Baker);
Trevor Bounford;
Alastair Campbell; Eikon Illustrations (Tony Dale, Robert Calow); Rebecca Johns; Sally Launder, Nicholas Rowland.

Photographs:
Francois Gohier (Ardea London); Carlos Goldin (Science Photo Library); P. J. Green (Ardea London); The Natural History Museum, London; Topham Picture-point; Adrian Warren (Ardea London).